LAVERNE MICKENS

Million Dollar Baby

How My Kids Won Millions Of Dollars In Scholarships & You Can Too!

The
Scholarship
College Mama

First edition

ISBN: 979-8-218-46187-4

This book was professionally typeset on Reedsy.
Find out more at reedsy.com

This book is dedicated to my family who love & support me.
To my husband Cory
And my five fabulous children
Kay, Kiara, Taylor, Joe, and Liz
Thank you for being my daily inspiration
I love you infinitely.

This book is also dedicated to my Scholarship Kids & Families
Thank you for trusting me and believing in me
Thank you for traveling this journey with me
If you follow me, booked a call, bought a product,
joined my live, attended a webinar, or asked for help...
Thank you. I appreciate you.

Contents

Introduction   1

1   CHAPTER 1: UNDERSTANDING SCHOLARSHIPS   5

2   CHAPTER 2: WHEN TO APPLY   10

3   CHAPTER 3: SEARCHING FOR SCHOLARSHIPS   13

4   CHAPTER 4: LOCAL SCHOLARSHIPS   17

5   CHAPTER 5: STATE SCHOLARSHIPS   21

6   CHAPTER 6: REGIONAL SCHOLARSHIPS   25

7   CHAPTER 7: NATIONAL SCHOLARSHIPS   30

8   CHAPTER 8: A WINNING APPLICATION   33

9   CHAPTER 9: CRAFTING AN AMAZ-
ING ESSAY   36

10   CHAPTER 10: CRAFTING YOUR RE-
SUME AND BRAG SHEET   40

11   CHAPTER 11 : SCHOLARSHIP INTERVIEWS   43

12   CHAPTER 12 : WINNING TIPS   49

13   CHAPTER 13 : SCHOLARSHIP
STACKING & DISPLACEMENT   52

14   CHAPTER 14 : MANAGING AND UTI-
LIZING YOUR SCHOLARSHIPS   54

15   CHAPTER 15 : HOW TO FIND NICHE
SCHOLARSHIPS JUST RIGHT FOR...   57

16   CHAPTER 16 : SCHOLARSHIPS FOR EVERYONE   61

17   CHAPTER 17 : SCHOLARSHIPS FOR
MARGINALIZED COMMUNITIES   67

18 CHAPTER 18: COMMUNITY COL-
    LEGE SCHOLARSHIPS & TRANSFER...   70
19 CHAPTER 19 : INTERNATIONAL SCHOLARSHIPS 74
20 CHAPTER 20 : SCHOLARSHIPS FOR
    STUDENTS WITH DISABILITIES   78
21 CHAPTER 21 : SCHOLARSHIPS FOR
    NON-TRADITIONAL STUDENTS &...   82
22 CHAPTER 22: SCHOLARSHIPS FOR
    HIGH SCHOOL STUDENTS   86
23 CHAPTER 23: SCHOLARSHIPS FOR
    COLLEGE STUDENTS   90
24 CHAPTER 24: GRADUATE SCHOLARSHIPS   94
25 Conclusion   98
Afterword   100
About the Author   101

Introduction

I began my scholarship journey in 1991 as a high school senior in Springfield, Massachusetts. I won 7 local scholarships and accessed my father's veteran benefits through the GI Bill. That got me through one year at Virginia State University. Then I had to return home. Without scholarships and grants to support me, I could not stay at an "out of state" HBCU that I had grown to love. No one told me what to do or showed me how to win scholarships. I had to struggle and find out on my own. I told myself if I ever had a family, I would not let my children struggle through this process.

Fast-forward to 2011, and I am preparing my oldest child to work on a college list, apply for internships, and apply for scholarships. It was sophomore year, by the way. I knew to start early. K. was a creative writing/game design aficionado. So, our first choice was Hampshire College. They didn't utilize traditional grades; we could create the major we wanted, and they were one of the first colleges to accept students as "test-optional." Hampshire was also 40 minutes away from us, which was a bonus. K. has sickle cell, and I knew I needed to be nearby

1

in a crisis. We were sold. Hampshire College's attendance cost in 2013 was $55,575, and we secured 75% of that in scholarships and grants. We graduated in 2018 debt-free.

Next up were my wonder twins, who were also academically excellent and highly motivated. They were also artists, which meant portfolios and auditions in addition to the Common App requirements. This also meant performing arts scholarships in addition to academic ones. Together in 2017, they secured over $500,000 in scholarships and grants, including Wendys, McDonald's, Burger King, Horatio Alger, Coca-Cola, and state, regional, and local scholarships. They are both graduates of Smith College and University of Amherst Massachusetts in 2021 and 2022. The twins are debt-free.

Then, there was Joe, who was very smart and curious but had no desire to be in school past 12th grade. Joe has also spent most of the year in the hospital due to sickle cell complications. College wasn't the goal; staying alive was. So, how surprised I was when Joe came home one afternoon and proudly proclaimed, "I GOT INTO COLLEGE!" It was mid-November, and Joe hadn't completed one application or written any personal statements. Joe didn't even have a Common App account. The community college reps visited the charter school that day, so Joe signed up and was accepted on-site. That was the pandemic year. Four years later, Joe is a college graduate with an associate's degree in culinary arts sciences. Joe is also debt-free.

Finally, we have the baby of the family, Elizabeth. I knew Liz would be the one to win all the accolades, grab all the headlines, and secure all the money. As an AP / Dual Enrollment student,

Liz graduated in 2023 third in her class with a 4.65 GPA and secured over $1 million in scholarships and grants. She was my fifth and final debt-free degree baby. That's when I knew I had to share my knowledge with others. The Scholarship College Mama was born.

Winning grants and scholarships is vital for students as they provide significant financial relief, allowing them to pursue higher education without the overwhelming debt burden. These financial aids cover tuition, books, and living expenses, making education more accessible, especially for those from low-income backgrounds. By alleviating financial stress, scholarships enable students to focus on their studies and extracurricular activities, leading to better academic performance and personal development. Additionally, winning scholarships can enhance a student's resume, showcasing their achievements and dedication, which can be advantageous when applying for jobs or further educational opportunities.

Applying for scholarships is equally essential as it opens the door to numerous opportunities that might otherwise be unavailable. The application process is a valuable experience, helping students develop essential skills such as writing, interviewing, and presenting their achievements. Scholarships can provide access to prestigious institutions and specialized programs significantly impacting a student's educational and career trajectory. Moreover, scholarships often come with networking opportunities, allowing recipients to connect with professionals, alums, and other scholars, fostering relationships that can benefit them throughout their careers. Ultimately, the effort invested in applying for scholarships can yield long-term benefits, contributing to a student's overall success and future opportunities.

Are you ready? Let's begin!

One

CHAPTER 1: UNDERSTANDING SCHOLARSHIPS

WHAT IS A SCHOLARSHIP

A scholarship is a financial award given to a student to help fund their education. Scholarships are typically awarded based on various criteria, such as academic merit, financial need, leadership qualities, or specific talents. Unlike loans, scholarships do not need to be repaid, making them a highly sought-after form of financial aid. They can cover various expenses, including tuition, books, and living costs. They can come from multiple sources, such as colleges, universities, private organizations, non-profits, and government agencies.

TYPES OF SCHOLARSHIPS

Several scholarships are available to students, each designed to meet different needs and recognize various achievements. Merit-based scholarships are awarded to students with exceptional academic performance, leadership skills, or artistic abilities. These scholarships often require a high GPA, strong test scores, and a record of extracurricular involvement. On the other hand, need-based scholarships are awarded to students who demonstrate financial need, assisting those who might not otherwise be able to afford higher education. Athletic scholarships are awarded to students who excel in sports, and they often come with the expectation that the student will compete for the school's athletic teams.

Additionally, there are scholarships aimed at specific demographics or fields of study. For example, scholarships for minority students, first-generation college students, or women in STEM fields aim to promote diversity and support underrepresented groups in higher education. Field-specific scholarships support students pursuing particular academic disciplines, such as engineering, medicine, or the arts. Some scholarships are also based on geographic location, helping students from specific regions or who plan to study in certain areas. By understanding the different types of scholarships available, students can better identify opportunities that align with their background, interests, and career goals, enhancing their chances of receiving financial support for their education.

SCHOLARSHIP MYTHS

1. SCHOLARSHIPS ARE ONLY FOR HIGH SCHOOL SENIORS

2. **SCHOLARSHIPS ARE ONLY FOR MINORITIES**
3. **YOU CAN ONLY APPLY TO SCHOLARSHIPS AFTER YOU ARE ACCEPTED**
4. **SCHOLARSHIPS ARE ONLY FOR STRAIGHT "A" STUDENTS**

THESE ARE ALL LIES AND MYTHS!

Numerous myths and misconceptions about scholarships can deter students from applying or pursuing them effectively. One common myth is that scholarships are only for straight-A students or those with exceptional athletic abilities. While academic and athletic scholarships exist and are competitive, countless other scholarships are available for various talents, interests, and backgrounds. Scholarships can be awarded based on community service, unique hobbies, leadership roles, or specific career goals, among other criteria. This misconception can prevent students from exploring the wide range of opportunities that might be a perfect fit for their profiles.

Another prevalent myth is that applying for scholarships is not worth the effort because the chances of winning are too slim. This belief often discourages students from applying, leading to missed opportunities. The truth is that many scholarships, mainly local or niche scholarships, receive fewer applications than expected. By taking the time to research and apply for various scholarships, students can significantly increase their chances of receiving financial aid. Additionally, some scholarships are renewable, meaning a successful application can provide financial support for multiple years of study.

A third myth is that scholarships are only for incoming first-year students, leaving upper-level students to rely solely on loans or other forms of financial aid. In reality, many scholarships are available for students at all stages of their college education, including those already enrolled. Scholars are specifically for sophomores, juniors, seniors, and graduate students. Students should continually search for and apply for scholarships throughout their academic careers to maximize their financial aid opportunities. Students can take full advantage of the financial resources available to support their educational goals by debunking these myths and understanding the actual landscape of scholarships.

MERIT AID SCHOLARSHIPS

Merit aid scholarships are financial awards granted to students based on their academic achievements, talents, or other exceptional abilities rather than financial need. These scholarships recognize high academic performance, athletics, artistic endeavors, or leadership. Typically, merit aid scholarships require a strong GPA, high standardized test scores, or a demonstrated track record of excellence in a particular field. Some merit scholarships may also consider extracurricular activities, community service, and personal achievements. By rewarding students for their accomplishments, merit aid scholarships not only help reduce the financial burden of education but also encourage continued excellence and motivation in their respective areas of talent.

FINANCIAL NEED-BASED SCHOLARSHIPS

Financial need-based scholarships are awards given to students primarily based on their financial situation and need for financial assistance to pursue higher education. These scholarships aim to bridge the gap between the cost of education and what a student's family can afford, making college accessible to those from lower-income backgrounds. Determining financial need typically involves an assessment of the family's income, assets, and other financial obligations, often through forms like the Free Application for Federal Student Aid (FAFSA). By providing crucial financial support, need-based scholarships help ensure that capable and motivated students can achieve their academic goals, regardless of their financial circumstances.

NOW LETS TALK ABOUT WHEN YOU SHOULD APPLY TO SCHOLARSHIPS!

Two

CHAPTER 2: WHEN TO APPLY

SCHOLARSHIPS ARE ALL YEAR-ROUND

Applying for scholarships is a year-round activity, and understanding the seasonal cycles and deadlines is crucial to maximizing your chances of securing financial aid. It's essential to start early, ideally during your junior year of high school, to identify and prepare for upcoming scholarship opportunities. Many prominent national scholarships have fall deadlines, typically from September to December, and require extensive applications that include essays, recommendation letters, and detailed personal information. Starting early gives you ample time to gather all the necessary documents and polish your application to stand out.

In addition to national scholarships, there are numerous scholarships with spring deadlines, often ranging from January to

April. These include many state and regional scholarships and those offered by specific colleges and universities. By staying organized and keeping a calendar of deadlines, you can ensure you don't miss out on these opportunities. It's also beneficial to regularly check scholarship databases, school bulletin boards, and community announcements for new scholarships that might become available throughout the year.

Summer is another critical time for scholarship applications, particularly for local and community-based scholarships. Many organizations, such as local businesses, non-profits, and civic groups, offer scholarships with deadlines in late spring or early summer. These scholarships often have fewer applicants than national awards, increasing your chances of winning. Utilizing the summer months to focus on these applications can be particularly advantageous, as you'll have more free time without the pressures of the school year.

Lastly, don't forget that scholarships are not just for incoming first-year students. Many scholarships are available for students already enrolled in college, with deadlines scattered throughout the academic year. Continuing to search for and apply for scholarships even after starting college can help alleviate financial stress and reduce the need for student loans. Maintaining a proactive approach and consistently looking for scholarship opportunities year-round can significantly increase your financial support and make your educational journey more affordable.

TIMELINE FOR SCHOLARSHIP APPLICATIONS

September to December

- National Scholarships: Applications open in September and close by December. It's essential to start early due to the extensive requirements.

January to April

- State Scholarships: Applications generally open in January and close by April. These are ideal for students looking to stay in-state for their education.

- Regional Scholarships: Similar to state scholarships, regional ones open in January and close by April. They often have specific eligibility criteria based on the region.

- College-Specific Scholarships: Many colleges offer scholarships starting in January, with deadlines typically in April.

March to June

- Local Scholarships: Applications open in March and close by June. These scholarships often have fewer applicants, increasing your chances of winning.

So, where do you look for scholarships? What are the best sites to research? Here are some of my favorite sites!

Three

CHAPTER 3: SEARCHING FOR SCHOLARSHIPS

WHERE TO SEARCH

Searching for scholarships requires a strategic approach to find the opportunities best suited to your needs and qualifications. One of the most effective ways to begin is by utilizing scholarship search engines and websites. These platforms allow you to input your personal information, academic achievements, and interests to generate a list of scholarships that match your profile. Websites like FastWeb, Scholarship.com, Scholarships 360, and Going Merry are famous for their comprehensive databases and user-friendly interfaces. Platforms like the College Board's Scholarship Search and JLV College Counseling also provide tailored recommendations based on your unique characteristics.

MY FAVORITE SCHOLARSHIP SEARCH SITES;

1. **Scholarship America**
2. **JLV College Counseling**
3. **Bold.org**
4. **Scholarships 360**
5. **Scholarships.com**
6. **Going Merry**
7. **MEFA**

In addition to online resources, high school, and community resources are vital in the scholarship search process. High school guidance counselors are often well-informed about local and regional scholarships that may not be listed on major search engines. They can provide valuable advice, application tips, and even letters of recommendation. Many high schools also host financial aid nights and scholarship workshops to help students navigate the application process. Community organizations, such as local rotary clubs, non-profits, and religious institutions, often offer scholarships to local students. These local opportunities can be less competitive than national scholarships, increasing the chances of receiving an award.

Utilizing a combination of online search engines and high school or community resources can significantly enhance your scholarship search strategy. Begin by creating profiles on multiple scholarship websites to access various opportunities. Regularly update your profiles and check for new scholarships. Simultaneously, engage with your high school guidance counselor and participate in community events to uncover local scholarships. By diversifying your approach and actively seeking out scholarships from various sources, you can maximize your chances of finding and securing the financial aid needed to support your educational journey.

HOW TO SEARCH

Searching for scholarships requires a systematic approach to ensure students maximize their opportunities. The first step is to use online scholarship search engines and databases, which can streamline the process by matching students with scholarships that fit their unique profiles. Scholarship websites allow students to create profiles detailing their academic achievements, interests, and backgrounds. These platforms then generate lists of potential scholarships tailored to the individual's qualifications. Regularly updating these profiles and setting reminders for application deadlines can help students stay organized and ensure they don't miss any opportunities.

In addition to online resources, students should leverage high school and community resources in their scholarship search. High school guidance counselors are invaluable sources of information, and they are often aware of local and regional scholarships that may not be widely advertised. These counselors can also provide support with the application process, including writing letters of recommendation and offering tips on crafting personal solid statements. Community organizations, such as local businesses, civic groups, and religious institutions, frequently offer scholarships to local students. Engaging with these groups, attending scholarship workshops, and networking within the community can uncover additional scholarship opportunities that might be less competitive than national awards. By combining online tools with local resources, students can cast a wide net and improve their chances of securing the financial aid needed for their education.

THE BEST WAY TO WIN IS THROUGH LOCAL SCHOLARSHIPS! LETS TALK ABOUT IT!

Four

CHAPTER 4: LOCAL SCHOLARSHIPS

WHAT ARE LOCAL SCHOLARSHIPS

Local scholarships are financial awards offered by organizations within a specific community or region, such as local businesses, community foundations, civic groups, and nonprofits. These scholarships are often tailored to benefit students who reside in the area, attend local schools, or are involved in community activities. Local scholarships can be a valuable resource for students as they tend to have fewer applicants than national scholarships, increasing the chances of winning. Additionally, they often emphasize community involvement and service, providing recognition for students' contributions to their local area.

Finding local scholarships requires a proactive approach. One of the best places to start is your high school guidance counselor's office, where information about local scholarship opportunities is frequently available. High schools often maintain lists of local scholarships and can provide details on application deadlines and requirements. Community bulletin boards, local newspapers, and newsletters are also excellent sources of information. Many local businesses and civic organizations announce scholarship opportunities through these channels. Additionally, visiting the websites of local foundations, businesses, and community groups can reveal scholarships that might not be widely advertised.

THE BENEFITS AND ADVANTAGES OF LOCAL SCHOLARSHIPS

The benefits of local scholarships extend beyond the financial support they provide. Winning a local scholarship often means gaining recognition within your community, which can open doors to networking opportunities and further support. Local scholarships may also be renewable, providing ongoing financial assistance throughout college. They often have more personalized selection criteria, considering factors such as community service, local involvement, and specific fields of study that benefit the community. This focus on local criteria can make it easier for students who may not have the highest academic scores but are deeply involved in their community to secure funding for their education.

Examples of local scholarships include awards from local Rotary clubs, chambers of commerce, and community foundations. For instance, the Rotary Club often offers scholarships to students with vital community service and leadership skills. The Chamber of Commerce in many towns provides scholarships to students pursuing business-related degrees or who plan to contribute to the local economy. Community foundations, like the Cleveland Foundation or the Silicon Valley Community Foundation, manage numerous local scholarships, each with specific eligibility criteria tailored to support students in their respective regions. By exploring these and other regional opportunities, students can find valuable financial resources to help fund their education while also receiving recognition for their community contributions.

WE WON OVER $30,000 IN LOCAL SCHOLARSHIPS!

1. **SEA Teachers Union**
2. **MLK Community Center**
3. **Pennies for Arts**
4. **Arrha Credit Union**
5. **PVCU Credit Union**
6. **The Ad Company**
7. **Springfield Partners for Community Action**
8. **Big Y Supermarkets**
9. **Caribbean Culture Club**
10. **Wesley United Methodist Church**
11. **Jewish Women's Council**
12. **Buffalo Soldiers of Western Mass**
13. **Western Mass News : TV 40 ABC**
14. **Zonta Women International**

Local scholarships have less competition and are lower amounts of money that can add up quickly! Great places to look include banks, credit unions, community foundations, churches, mosques, synagogues, grocery stores, rotary clubs, unions, and more!

COMMUNITY FOUNDATIONS GIVE LOCAL SCHOLARSHIPS

Community foundations are nonprofit organizations that manage charitable funds from individuals, families, and businesses to support local initiatives and projects, including scholarships. These foundations play a crucial role in awarding local scholarships by pooling resources to create endowments that provide ongoing financial support for students within the community. Community foundations typically offer a variety of scholarships with specific eligibility criteria, such as academic achievement, financial need, field of study, or community involvement. The application process for these scholarships often includes submitting essays, recommendation letters, and academic transcripts. By collaborating with local donors and organizations, community foundations ensure that scholarship funds are distributed to deserving students, helping them pursue higher education and contribute to the community's growth and development.

NOW LETS TALK ABOUT STATE SCHOLARSHIPS!

Five

CHAPTER 5: STATE SCHOLARSHIPS

❧

S TATE SCHOLARSHIP OPPORTUNITIES

State scholarships are financial awards state governments provide to support residents pursuing higher education within the state. These scholarships encourage students to attend in-state colleges and universities, fostering a more educated workforce and contributing to the state's economic development. State scholarships often prioritize academic excellence, financial need, or specific fields of study that align with the state's strategic goals. They can significantly reduce the cost of tuition, making college more affordable and accessible to a broader range of students.

Each state offers scholarship programs, often with unique eligibility requirements and application processes. For instance, the Georgia HOPE Scholarship rewards high school students with vital academic records by covering a substantial portion of their tuition costs at eligible Georgia colleges and universities. Similarly, the California Cal Grant program provides financial aid based on GPA and financial need, helping students from low and middle-income families. Many states also offer scholarships for students pursuing careers in high-demand fields such as teaching, nursing, and STEM (science, technology, engineering, and mathematics).

State-specific resources are available to help students identify and apply for these scholarships. State education department websites typically provide comprehensive scholarship information, including eligibility criteria, application deadlines, and required documentation. High school guidance counselors and college financial aid offices are valuable resources for students seeking state scholarships. Additionally, many states have dedicated scholarship search platforms and online portals where students can submit their applications and track their status.

Case studies of successful state scholarship applications highlight the importance of thorough preparation and adherence to application guidelines. For example, a student from Texas who applied for the Texas Grant program meticulously documented their financial need and academic achievements, resulting in a full tuition scholarship. Another student in New York, aiming for the Excelsior Scholarship, ensured they met all educational and residency requirements and submitted a compelling essay on their commitment to contributing to the state's workforce. These success stories demonstrate that with careful planning and attention to detail, students can effectively leverage state scholarship opportunities to fund their education and achieve their academic goals.

STATE SCHOLARSHIP EXAMPLES NATIONWIDE

1. California | Cal Grant | Based on GPA and financial need; covers tuition costs
2. Georgia | HOPE Scholarship | Rewards academic excellence; covers tuition for in-state students
3. New York | Excelsior Scholarship | Covers full tuition for in-state public colleges for eligible students
4. Texas | Texas Grant | Provides grants to students with financial need; covers tuition
5. Florida | Bright Futures Scholarship | Merit-based scholarship; covers tuition and fees
6. Illinois | Illinois Monetary Award Program (MAP) | Need-based grant; provides financial aid to eligible students
7. Michigan | Michigan Competitive Scholarship | Need-based; provides financial assistance to eligible students
8. Carolina | North Carolina Education Lottery Scholarship | Lottery-funded; offers financial aid to in-state students
9. Ohio | Ohio College Opportunity Grant | Need-based grant; supports low-income students
10. Pennsylvania | Pennsylvania State Grant | Need-based grant; covers tuition and fees for eligible students

These state scholarships offer various forms of financial aid, making higher education more accessible and affordable for students within their respective states.

NEXT UP: REGIONAL SCHOLARSHIPS!

Six

CHAPTER 6: REGIONAL SCHOLARSHIPS

WHAT ARE REGIONAL SCHOLARSHIPS

Regional scholarships are financial awards provided to students within a specific geographic area, such as a cluster of states, a single state, or even a particular county or city. These scholarships are designed to support students who reside or attend school in a defined region, often reflecting the commitment of local organizations and foundations to invest in the education and future of their communities. The scope of regional scholarships can vary significantly, covering tuition, books, and other educational expenses. They are typically less competitive than national scholarships, offering better chances for local students to secure funding.

Key organizations and foundations play a crucial role in offering regional scholarships. For example, the New England Regional Student Program provides tuition breaks for students from New England states attending participating institutions. Similarly, the Western Undergraduate Exchange offers reduced tuition rates for students from participating western states. Foundations like the Silicon Valley Community Foundation and the Cleveland Foundation offer scholarships tailored to students in their respective regions, emphasizing local community service, academic achievement, and leadership potential. These organizations often collaborate with local businesses, educational institutions, and community leaders to fund and manage scholarship programs.

Success stories from regional scholarship winners highlight the significant impact these awards can have on students' educational journeys. One such story is that of a student from rural Georgia who received a scholarship from the Community Foundation of Central Georgia. This award enabled her to attend a prestigious state university without the burden of debt, allowing her to focus on her studies and extracurricular activities. Another inspiring example is a student from the Pacific Northwest who benefited from the Horatio Alger Association's regional scholarship program. This scholarship provided the financial support needed to pursue a degree in engineering, leading to internships and job offers that set the stage for a successful career.

These success stories illustrate the transformative power of regional scholarships in terms of financial assistance and providing encouragement and validation to students. Regional scholarships help foster community and support by focusing on students within a specific area, ensuring that local talent is nurtured and developed. They often require applicants to demonstrate a commitment to their community through service or leadership, reinforcing the values of giving back and civic responsibility. As such, regional scholarships play a vital role in helping students achieve their educational goals while strengthening their local communities' fabric.

EXAMPLES OF REGIONAL SCHOLARSHIPS

Here are examples of regional scholarships available nationwide:

Western United States
  1. Western Undergraduate Exchange (WUE)
  - Region: Western states (e.g., California, Arizona, Washington)
  - Description: Offers reduced tuition rates for students from participating western states attending participating institutions.

2. Horatio Alger Association Regional Scholarships
  - Region: Various regions within the Western U.S.
  - Description: Provides financial aid to students who have faced significant adversity and demonstrate financial need and a commitment to pursuing higher education.

Midwest United States
  3. Community Foundation of Greater Des Moines Scholarships

- Region: Central Iowa
- Description: Offers various scholarships for students from central Iowa, emphasizing community involvement and academic achievement.

4. Great Lakes National Scholarship Program
   - Region: Great Lakes states (e.g., Illinois, Michigan, Ohio)
   - Description: Awards scholarships to students pursuing STEM degrees within the Great Lakes region.

Southern United States
   5. Community Foundation of Central Georgia Scholarships
   - Region: Central Georgia
   - Description: Provides a range of scholarships for students in central Georgia, supporting academic excellence and community service.

6. Tennessee HOPE Scholarship
   - Region: Tennessee
   - Description: Offers scholarships to Tennessee residents based on academic achievement, supporting attendance at in-state colleges and universities.

Northeastern United States
   7. New England Regional Student Program
   - Region: New England states (e.g., Massachusetts, Maine, Vermont)
   - Description: Provides tuition breaks for students from New England states attending participating regional institutions.

8. Daughters of the American Revolution (DAR) Massachusetts

Scholarships
  - Region: Massachusetts
  - Description: Offers scholarships to students residing in Massachusetts, focusing on academic achievement and community service.

Southeastern United States
  9. Central Florida Community Foundation Scholarships
  - Region: Central Florida
  - Description: Provides scholarships to students from central Florida, supporting various fields of study and community engagement.

10. North Carolina Community Foundation Scholarships
  - Region: North Carolina
  - Description: Offers multiple scholarships for students across North Carolina, with various eligibility criteria based on academic achievement and community involvement.

These regional scholarships offer diverse opportunities for students to secure financial aid based on their geographic location, community involvement, academic achievements, and specific fields of study. Students can find scholarships tailored to their unique backgrounds and goals by exploring these options.

NOW LETS TALK ABOUT NATIONAL SCHOLARSHIPS!

Seven

CHAPTER 7: NATIONAL SCHOLARSHIPS

~~~

WHAT ARE NATIONAL SCHOLARSHIPS?

National scholarships are prestigious financial awards offered to students nationwide, providing significant financial support to help cover the cost of higher education. These scholarships are typically sponsored by large organizations, corporations, and foundations, and they often come with substantial monetary awards that can cover tuition, fees, books, and sometimes even living expenses. Because of their broad eligibility, national scholarships are highly competitive, attracting applicants from diverse backgrounds and regions. Winning a national scholarship alleviates financial burdens and adds significant value to a student's resume, often opening doors to further academic and professional opportunities.

Major national scholarship programs include the Coca-Cola Scholars Program, the Gates Millennium Scholars Program, the National Merit Scholarship, and the Jack Kent Cooke Foundation Scholarship. The Coca-Cola Scholars Program awards 150 scholarships yearly to high school seniors who demonstrate academic excellence, leadership, and community service. The Gates Millennium Scholars Program provides full financial support to minority students with significant financial needs who exhibit strong academic and leadership potential. Based on PSAT/NMSQT scores, the National Merit Scholarship recognizes the top 1% of high school students nationwide. The Jack Kent Cooke Foundation Scholarship supports high-achieving students with financial needs, offering undergraduate and graduate studies funding.

NATIONAL SCHOLARSHIP CRITERIA

Given the high level of competition, the criteria for national scholarships are often stringent and multifaceted. Applicants are typically evaluated on their academic performance, including GPA and standardized test scores, as well as their extracurricular activities, leadership roles, and community service. Personal essays, letters of recommendation, and sometimes interviews are crucial components of the application process. Scholarships like the National Merit Scholarship rely heavily on test scores. At the same time, programs like the Gates Millennium Scholars Program emphasize a combination of academic achievements and leadership qualities, particularly among minority and underrepresented groups.

HOW TO STAND OUT ON A NATIONAL LEVEL

Students should focus on compellingly showcasing their unique strengths and experiences to stand out nationally. This includes maintaining a high GPA, excelling in standardized tests, actively participating in extracurricular activities, assuming leadership roles, and demonstrating initiative and impact. Crafting a standout personal essay is essential; applicants should tell a compelling story highlighting their passion, resilience, and commitment to their goals and securing solid letters of recommendation from teachers, mentors, or community leaders who can attest to the student's qualifications and character. Finally, students should thoroughly research each scholarship program's specific criteria and tailor their applications to align with its values and objectives, enhancing their chances of success.

NATIONAL SCHOLARSHIPS MY CHILDREN HAVE WON

1. **Dell Scholars**
2. **Hagan Foundation**
3. **Wendys High School Heisman**
4. **Burger King Scholars**
5. **McDonald's Scholars**
6. **ELKS Most Valuable Students Award**
7. **Horatio Alger Scholars**

Let your PASSION shine through and show us all your "IT" factor!

Now, how do you create an award-winning application?

Eight

CHAPTER 8: A WINNING APPLICATION

꩜

HOW TO CREATE A WINNING APPLICATION

Creating a winning scholarship application involves careful planning, attention to detail, and a strategic approach to highlighting your strengths and achievements. Essential components of a scholarship application typically include a well-written personal essay, letters of recommendation, academic transcripts, and a resume or list of extracurricular activities. The personal essay is a critical element where you can showcase your personality, experiences, and aspirations, providing a narrative that connects your background to the goals of the scholarship. Letters of recommendation should come from individuals who know you well and can speak to your accomplishments and character, such as teachers, mentors, or community leaders. Academic transcripts record your academic performance, while the resume outlines your extracurricular involvement, leadership roles, and any relevant work or volunteer experience.

AVOID ANY MISTAKES

Avoiding common application mistakes is crucial to creating a solid application. One common mistake is missing deadlines, which can be easily avoided by making a detailed calendar of all scholarship deadlines and setting reminders. Another mistake is submitting incomplete applications; ensure all required documents and information are included before submitting. Failing to follow instructions is another pitfall—each scholarship may have specific requirements, such as word limits for essays or formatting guidelines, and adhering to these is essential. Additionally, generic applications not tailored to the particular scholarship can hurt your chances; make sure each application is personalized and clearly shows why you are a good fit for that specific award.

STAY ORGANIZED

To stay organized and ensure you don't miss any crucial steps, follow a detailed checklist for scholarship applications. Start by researching and identifying scholarships that match your profile and goals. Gather all necessary documents, including transcripts, recommendation letters, and a resume. Write and revise your essay, ensuring it's tailored to each scholarship and highlights your unique qualities and experiences. Double-check all application instructions and requirements, and review each component for accuracy and completeness. Having someone else review your application to catch errors or provide feedback is also helpful. Finally, submit your application before the deadline to avoid any last-minute issues.

Focusing on these essential components, avoiding common mistakes, and following a detailed checklist can help you create a compelling and organized scholarship application. This approach increases your chances of winning scholarships and demonstrates your dedication and attention to detail, qualities that scholarship committees highly value. Preparing and polishing your application thoroughly can make a significant difference in securing the financial aid needed to achieve your educational goals.

Nine

CHAPTER 9: CRAFTING AN AMAZING ESSAY

❦

PAINT A PICTURE AND TELL YOUR STORY

Writing a compelling scholarship essay starts with a thorough understanding of the prompt. Carefully read the prompt to grasp what the scholarship committee is asking for. Identify the key themes and any specific questions that need to be addressed. Understanding the prompt helps you stay focused and ensures your essay meets the requirements. It's also important to consider the values and goals of the organization offering the scholarship, as aligning your response with these can make your application stand out.

Brainstorming and outlining your essay are crucial steps in the writing process. Begin by jotting down all your ideas related to the prompt. Think about your experiences, achievements, and challenges related to the essay topic. Once you have a list of ideas, organize them coherently. An outline will help you arrange your thoughts logically and ensure your essay flows smoothly. Typically, a scholarship essay should have an introduction, body paragraphs, and a conclusion. Use the outline to determine the main points you want to make in each section and how they connect to the overall theme.

HOOK THEM IN!

Grab the reader's attention right away! The same way you scroll past a boring Instagram or TikTok video is how judges will grow tired of your writing and put you in the "NO" pile. Writing a compelling introduction is essential to grab the reader's attention. Start with a hook, such as an interesting anecdote, a surprising fact, or a provocative question. This sets the tone for your essay and engages the reader from the beginning. Clearly state your central thesis or the purpose of your essay in the introduction. This thesis should succinctly convey the central message you want to communicate. The introduction should be concise yet powerful, setting up the rest of your essay effectively.

Developing strong body paragraphs involves elaborating on the critical points outlined. Each paragraph should focus on a single idea or aspect of your story. Use specific examples and details to illustrate your points, making your essay more vivid and personal. Show, don't just tell—use anecdotes and experiences to demonstrate your achievements and challenges. Ensure each paragraph transitions smoothly to the next, maintaining a logical flow. This coherence helps keep the reader engaged and makes your essay more persuasive.

Crafting a memorable conclusion is as vital as the introduction. Summarize the main points of your essay, reinforcing how they address the prompt and align with the scholarship's values. Reflect on what you've learned from your experiences and how the scholarship will help you achieve your goals. End with a strong closing statement that leaves a lasting impression, such as a call to action or a hopeful vision for the future.

GET FRESH EYES ON YOUR WRITING

Editing and proofreading your essay is vital to ensure it is polished and error-free. After writing your first draft, take a break before revising to approach your work with fresh eyes. Check for grammatical errors, awkward phrasing, and clarity. It can be helpful to read your essay aloud or have someone else review it to catch mistakes you might have missed. Consider feedback carefully and make revisions to improve the essay's quality.

Sample essays and analysis can provide valuable insights into what makes a victorious scholarship essay. Analyzing examples of winning essays can help you understand how to structure your own, what kinds of stories resonate with scholarship committees, and how to convey your message effectively. Look for essays that align with the types of scholarships you are applying for, note the techniques used to engage the reader, and articulate the writer's goals and experiences.

By following these tips—understanding the prompt, brainstorming and outlining, writing a compelling introduction, developing strong body paragraphs, crafting a memorable conclusion, and thoroughly editing and proofreading—you can create a powerful scholarship essay that stands out. Utilizing sample essays for inspiration and analysis further enhances your ability to craft a winning essay that effectively communicates your unique strengths and aspirations.

MY ESSAY WRITING TIPS INCLUDE;

1. **Use vivid vocabulary**
2. **Use simile, metaphor, and personification**
3. **Hook them in within the first paragraph**
4. **Use a witty story, clever saying, song lyric, or movie phrase**
5. **Get fresh eyes to edit your writing**
6. **Do not write how you talk or how you text; don't be familiar**
7. **Tell your story and paint a picture for the judges**

Ten

CHAPTER 10: CRAFTING YOUR RESUME AND BRAG SHEET

C rafting a winning scholarship resume and brag sheet is essential for showcasing your achievements and qualifications in a structured and compelling manner. A scholarship resume should include your personal information, academic achievements, extracurricular activities, work experience, community service, skills, and any awards or honors you have received. Start with your name, contact information, and a brief objective or summary statement highlighting your educational and career goals. Under academic achievements, list your GPA, standardized test scores, relevant coursework, and any academic honors. Extracurricular activities should detail your involvement in clubs, sports, arts, and other interests, emphasizing leadership roles and significant contributions.

CHAPTER 10: CRAFTING YOUR RESUME AND BRAG SHEET

Formatting your scholarship resume correctly can make a big difference. Use a clean, professional layout with clear headings and bullet points to organize information logically. Choose a simple, readable font such as Arial or Times New Roman, and keep the font size between 10 and 12 points. Ensure consistent formatting throughout the document, including uniform date formats and aligned text. Limit your resume to one page unless you have extensive experience that justifies a second page. Remember to include action verbs to describe your achievements and responsibilities, such as "led," "organized," "achieved," and "volunteered," to convey your accomplishments effectively.

Creating a brag sheet is a complementary process to crafting your resume and is particularly useful for scholarship applications that require letters of recommendation. A brag sheet provides a comprehensive list of your achievements, activities, skills, and personal traits to help recommenders write detailed and specific letters. Include sections on your academic achievements, extracurricular activities, volunteer work, work experience, awards, and personal goals. Unlike a resume, a brag sheet can be more descriptive, providing context and anecdotes highlighting your strengths and character. For example, you might describe a project you led, its impact, and what you learned from the experience.

Examples and templates can guide you in creating an effective scholarship resume and brag sheet. Many educational websites and career services offer templates specifically designed for students. For instance, a scholarship resume template might feature sections for personal information, education, activities, and awards, with prompts to help you fill in each part. Similarly, brag sheet templates often include detailed questions to help you think about and articulate your achievements. These templates ensure you cover all essential areas and professionally present your information. Reviewing examples of successful scholarship resumes and brag sheets can provide inspiration and a benchmark for your documents.

You can craft a compelling scholarship resume and brag sheet by including all relevant information, following formatting best practices, and using templates and examples for guidance. These documents highlight your qualifications and demonstrate your organization and attention to detail, qualities that scholarship committees highly value. With a well-prepared resume and brag sheet, you can effectively communicate your achievements and potential, significantly enhancing your chances of securing scholarships.

Eleven

CHAPTER 11 : SCHOLARSHIP INTERVIEWS

⁓⚮⁓

P reparing for a scholarship interview requires thorough preparation and practice to ensure you make a positive and lasting impression. Start by researching the scholarship organization to understand its mission, values, and the qualities it seeks in candidates. This knowledge will help you tailor your responses to the organization's expectations. Review your application materials, including your resume, personal statement, and any essays you submitted, as interviewers often ask questions based on this information. Familiarize yourself with your achievements and experiences so that you can discuss them confidently and coherently.

Scholarship interviews can take various formats, including one-on-one, panel, or group interviews. In a one-on-one interview, you will speak directly with a single interviewer, which allows for a more personalized and in-depth conversation. Panel interviews involve multiple interviewers asking questions, requiring you to engage with several people simultaneously. Group interviews, less common, involve multiple candidates interviewed together, testing your ability to interact and stand out in a group setting. Understanding the format in advance can help you prepare mentally and strategically for the interview process.

Preparing answers to common scholarship interview questions is essential. Typical questions might include "Tell me about yourself," "Why do you deserve this scholarship?" "What are your career goals?" and "How have you demonstrated leadership or overcome challenges?" Develop thoughtful, concise answers highlighting your achievements, experiences, and aspirations. Use the STAR method (Situation, Task, Action, Result) to structure your responses, ensuring you provide specific examples and precise outcomes. Practice answering these questions aloud to build confidence and fluency.

Making a strong impression during the interview involves several vital strategies. Dress professionally to convey respect and seriousness about the opportunity. Arrive early to demonstrate punctuality and eagerness. During the interview, maintain good posture and eye contact, and listen attentively to each question. Speak clearly and confidently, and avoid filler words such as "um" and "like." Show enthusiasm for the scholarship and express gratitude for the opportunity to interview. Mock interviews can be incredibly beneficial in preparing for the real thing. Ask a teacher, mentor, or friend to conduct a practice interview and provide feedback on your performance.

Follow-up etiquette is also crucial in the scholarship interview process. After the interview, send a thank-you email to the interviewers, expressing your appreciation for their time and consideration. Mention specific aspects of the interview that you enjoyed or found particularly meaningful, reinforcing your interest in the scholarship. This polite and professional gesture can leave a positive impression and keep you fresh in the interviewers' minds. By preparing thoroughly, practicing diligently, and demonstrating professionalism and enthusiasm, you can excel in your scholarship interview and significantly enhance your chances of receiving the award.

Outline: Preparing for a Scholarship Interview (In Person and Online)

I. Pre-Interview Preparation
  1. Research the Scholarship Organization
  - Understand the organization's mission, values, and goals.
  - Know the specific criteria and qualities they are looking for in candidates.

2. Review Your Application Materials
  - Revisit your resume, personal statement, and essays.
  - Be prepared to discuss any part of your application in detail.

3. Understand the Interview Format
  - Identify whether the interview will be one-on-one, panel, or group.
  - Prepare accordingly for the specific format.

II. Preparing Answers to Common Questions

1. Typical Interview Questions
- Tell me about yourself.
- Why do you deserve this scholarship?
- What are your career goals?
- How have you demonstrated leadership or overcome challenges?

2. Using the STAR Method
- Situation: Describe the context within which you performed a task or faced a challenge.
- Task: Explain the actual task or challenge involved.
- Action: Describe your specific actions to address the task or challenge.
- Result: Share the outcomes or results of your actions.

III. Mock Interview Practice
1. Conducting Mock Interviews
- Ask a teacher, mentor, or friend to role-play as the interviewer.
- Practice answering questions aloud to build confidence.
- Request feedback on your performance and areas for improvement.

2. Simulating Interview Conditions
- For in-person interviews: Practice sitting upright, making eye contact, and speaking clearly.
- For online interviews: Ensure your technology works, practice using the platform, and set up a quiet, professional-looking background.

IV. Day of the Interview (In Person)

CHAPTER 11 : SCHOLARSHIP INTERVIEWS

1. Dress Professionally
- Choose appropriate, professional attire that reflects the seriousness of the occasion.

2. Arrive Early
- Plan to arrive at least 15 minutes early to account for any unforeseen delays.
- Use the extra time to relax and compose yourself.

3. Bring Necessary Materials
- Copies of your resume, application materials, and a notepad with questions for the interviewers.

4. During the Interview
- Maintain good posture, make eye contact, and listen attentively.
- Speak clearly and confidently, and avoid filler words.

V. Day of the Interview (Online)
1. Test Your Technology
- Ensure your internet connection is stable.
- Test your webcam, microphone, and any necessary software or platforms.

2. Set Up a Professional Environment
- Choose a quiet, well-lit space with a clean, professional background.
- Minimize potential interruptions from family members, pets, or electronic devices.

3. Dress Professionally

- Dress as you would for an in-person interview, from head to toe.

4. During the Interview
   - Look directly at the camera to simulate eye contact.
   - Maintain good posture and speak clearly, ensuring concise and articulate responses.

VI. Post-Interview Follow-Up
   1. Send a Thank-You Note
   - Send a thank-you email to each interviewer within 24 hours.
   - Express your gratitude for the opportunity and mention meaningful aspects of the interview.

2. Reflect on Your Performance
   - Consider what went well and what could be improved for future interviews.
   - Take notes on any feedback received for continuous improvement.

This structured approach will help you prepare thoroughly for in-person and online scholarship interviews, increasing your chances of making a positive and lasting impression.

Twelve

CHAPTER 12 : WINNING TIPS

PERSONALIZE YOUR APPLICATION

Winning numerous scholarships requires a strategic and personalized approach to each application. One essential tip is personalizing your applications to fit each scholarship's criteria and values. Generic applications that do not address the particular questions or criteria of the scholarship often get overlooked. Review each scholarship thoroughly and tailor your application materials to reflect how your background, achievements, and goals align with what the scholarship committee seeks. Highlight relevant experiences and explain why you are an ideal candidate for that particular scholarship, demonstrating a genuine interest in their mission and values.

CREATE THE NARRATIVE

Building a solid narrative is another crucial element of a successful scholarship application. Your story should be compelling and coherent, combining your experiences, challenges, and aspirations. Use your essays to weave a narrative that showcases your journey, including any obstacles you have overcome and how they have shaped your ambitions. A well-crafted story makes your application memorable and helps the scholarship committee understand your motivations and future goals. Ensure your narrative demonstrates growth, resilience, and a clear vision of how the scholarship will help you achieve your objectives.

WHAT IS YOUR "IT" FACTOR

Showcasing your uniqueness is essential in standing out from the competition. Highlight what makes you different, whether it's a particular skill, passion, or experience that sets you apart. Emphasize unique achievements or projects that demonstrate your initiative and impact. For example, if you started a community service project or led a significant initiative at your school, these are excellent points to highlight. Your goal is to show the scholarship committee why you are not just a strong candidate but an exceptional one, bringing a unique perspective and contribution to their program.

SECURE STRONG RECOMMENDATIONS

Leveraging strong recommendation letters can significantly boost your scholarship applications. Choose recommenders who know you well and can provide detailed and enthusiastic support for your application. Provide them with a copy of your resume and a brief overview of the scholarship and your goals so they can tailor their letters accordingly. Consistency and persistence are also crucial. Applying for scholarships is a numbers game; the more you use, the better your chances. Keep a detailed calendar of deadlines, stay organized, and don't get discouraged by rejections. Each application is an opportunity to refine your approach and improve. By remaining persistent and consistently putting in the effort, you can increase your chances of winning multiple scholarships.

Thirteen

CHAPTER 13 : SCHOLARSHIP STACKING & DISPLACEMENT

⚜

Scholarship stacking refers to combining multiple scholarship awards to cover a more significant portion of educational expenses. This can include scholarships from various sources, such as federal, state, institutional, and private organizations. Scholarship stacking is advantageous because it can substantially reduce out-of-pocket costs for tuition, books, and other fees. However, careful management is required to ensure that the combined funds do not exceed the total cost of attendance, as this can sometimes lead to complications with financial aid packages.

On the other hand, scholarship displacement occurs when the total amount of scholarship funds a student receives exceeds their financial need or the cost of attendance, prompting the institution to reduce other forms of financial aid. For example, if a student is awarded multiple scholarships surpassing the calculated financial need, the school might reduce grants, loans, or work-study funds accordingly. This policy is intended to prevent over-awarding, but it can be frustrating for students who might lose out on anticipated financial aid.

Students should first understand their school's policies on external scholarships and financial aid adjustments to avoid scholarship displacement. Many schools have different approaches to handling excess scholarship funds. Some might apply the excess to future semesters, while others might reduce institutional aid. Students can understand how their scholarships will be treated and plan accordingly by discussing with the financial aid office. Focusing on need- and merit-based scholarships can help balance the total financial assistance package more effectively.

Another strategy to mitigate scholarship displacement is to prioritize scholarships that explicitly state they can be used for educational expenses beyond tuition, such as room and board, books, and supplies. This flexibility can help ensure that excess funds do not inadvertently reduce other aid forms. Additionally, maintaining communication with scholarship providers about how their funds are being utilized can sometimes result in the possibility of deferring or reallocating funds to avoid displacement. By staying informed and proactive, students can maximize their scholarship benefits and minimize the risk of financial aid adjustments.

Fourteen

CHAPTER 14 : MANAGING AND UTILIZING YOUR SCHOLARSHIPS

❧

M anaging and utilizing scholarship money effectively is crucial for maximizing the financial benefits and ensuring you can cover all necessary educational expenses. One key aspect is understanding the scholarship turnaround time, which refers to the period from application submission to receiving the funds. This can vary significantly between different scholarships. Some awards are disbursed before the start of the academic term, while others might be provided after the term begins. It's essential to keep track of these timelines to plan accordingly and ensure that you have the necessary funds available when you need them.

Handling multiple scholarships requires careful organization and strategic planning. If you are fortunate enough to receive numerous awards, you need to understand the terms and conditions of each scholarship. Some scholarships may stipulate how the funds can be used, such as covering only tuition or being applied to books and supplies. Additionally, some scholarships, known as a scholarship displacement policy, might reduce the amount of other financial aid you are eligible for. Keep detailed records of each scholarship, including the amount, disbursement schedule, and specific requirements. Communicating with your school's financial aid office can help you navigate these complexities and maximize the benefits of each award.

Budgeting and financial planning are critical components of effectively utilizing scholarship money. Create a comprehensive budget that outlines your anticipated educational expenses, including tuition, fees, books, supplies, and living costs. Compare this budget against the total scholarship funds you will receive. If there is a shortfall, identify other funding sources or consider ways to reduce your expenses. Maintaining a budget helps you manage your funds throughout the academic year, ensuring you do not run out of money mid-term. Additionally, setting aside some of your scholarship funds for unexpected expenses can provide a cushion and help you avoid financial stress.

Reporting scholarship awards is another crucial aspect of managing your funds. Many institutions require you to report any external scholarships you receive to the financial aid office. This is crucial for maintaining transparency and accurately adjusting your financial assistance package. Failure to report scholarships can lead to complications, such as owing money back to the school or losing eligibility for certain types of aid. When reporting scholarships, provide all necessary documentation and keep copies for your records. Communicating with your financial aid office and promptly reporting any changes can help you manage your scholarship funds efficiently and avoid potential issues.

Fifteen

CHAPTER 15 : HOW TO FIND NICHE SCHOLARSHIPS JUST RIGHT FOR YOU

F inding niche scholarships can significantly increase your chances of securing financial aid, as these scholarships are often targeted at specific groups or fields, resulting in less competition than more general scholarships. Here are several strategies to help you identify and apply for niche scholarships:

1. Identify Your Unique Qualities and Interests
   Start by listing your unique characteristics, interests, and experiences. Consider factors such as your:
   - Field of study or career aspirations
   - Hobbies and extracurricular activities
   - Ethnic or cultural background

- Membership in specific organizations (e.g., scouts, honor societies)
- Personal experiences or challenges (e.g., being a first-generation college student)
- Geographic location or residency

2. Use Specialized Scholarship Search Engines

Several scholarship search engines allow you to filter scholarships based on specific criteria. Websites like Going Merry, Scholarships.com, JLV College Counseling, and Bold Scholarships have advanced search features that let you input detailed information about yourself to find scholarships that match your profile.

3. Leverage Professional Associations and Organizations

Many professional associations and industry-specific organizations offer scholarships to students pursuing careers in their fields. For example:

- The National Society of Black Engineers (NSBE) offers scholarships to students studying engineering.
- The American Marketing Association (AMA) provides scholarships for marketing students.
- The National Association of Hispanic Journalists (NAHJ) awards scholarships to aspiring journalists.

4. Explore Local Community Resources

Check with local organizations, businesses, and community foundations for scholarships targeted at residents or students in your area. Local chambers of commerce, rotary clubs, and community foundations often offer scholarships to support local students.

5. Consult School and University Resources

Your high school guidance counselor or college financial aid office can be valuable resources for finding niche scholarships. They often have information about scholarships specific to your school, district, or region. Many colleges and universities also offer scholarships for particular majors, student groups, or departmental achievements.

6. Utilize Online Communities and Forums

Online forums and communities like Pinterest or Reddit can help discover niche scholarships. These platforms allow you to connect with other students, share opportunities, and get advice on the application process.

7. Research Scholarship Databases and Books

Books and databases dedicated to scholarships can be a treasure trove of information. Titles like "The Ultimate Scholarship Book" provide comprehensive lists of scholarships, including niche opportunities. Additionally, many libraries have access to databases that can help you find scholarships based on your specific criteria.

8. Contact Professional Networks and Mentors

Engage with your mentors, professional networks, and academic advisors. They can often point you toward niche scholarships related to your study or career path. Networking with professionals in your desired industry can also uncover lesser-known scholarship opportunities.

Combining these strategies allows you to uncover a wide

range of niche scholarships tailored to your unique profile. The more specific and targeted your search, the higher your chances of finding scholarships that fit your qualifications and reduce the overall competition. Stay organized, keep track of deadlines, and apply consistently to maximize your scholarship opportunities.

Sixteen

CHAPTER 16 : SCHOLARSHIPS FOR EVERYONE

S cholarships for non-minority students, including white and American students of European descent, are plentiful and encompass a wide range of criteria and fields of study. These scholarships are typically merit-based, need-based, or focused on specific talents and interests. Merit-based scholarships reward academic excellence, leadership, and extracurricular involvement, while need-based scholarships provide financial aid to students from lower-income families. Additionally, many scholarships are available for students pursuing particular majors, such as STEM fields, humanities, or the arts, ensuring that there are opportunities for all students regardless of their background.

One of the critical resources for finding scholarships available to non-minority students is using scholarship search engines like Fastweb, Scholarships.com, and Cappex. These platforms allow students to create profiles and receive personalized scholarship matches based on their academic achievements, interests, and career goals. High school guidance counselors and college financial aid offices are also valuable sources of information, offering access to databases and specific scholarship opportunities that might not be widely advertised. Additionally, local community organizations, businesses, and foundations often provide scholarships to students within their region or who are committed to their community.

Winning scholarships is possible for all students by following a strategic approach. Personalizing each application to align with the scholarship's criteria and demonstrating how your achievements, experiences, and aspirations make you an ideal candidate is essential. Crafting compelling personal essays, securing solid letters of recommendation, and maintaining a strong academic record are crucial steps in the application process. Furthermore, students should start their scholarship search early and apply for a wide range of scholarships to increase their chances of success. Persistence and consistency in applying are essential, as each application is an opportunity to refine your approach and improve your chances of winning.

Scholarships are open and available to all students, regardless of race, ethnicity, or background. They provide an essential means of making higher education accessible and affordable. By recognizing that scholarships are designed to support a diverse range of students, from those with high academic achievements to those with specific talents or financial needs, it's clear that everyone has opportunities. The availability of numerous scholarships ensures that every student has the potential to secure financial aid, thereby enabling them to pursue their educational and career aspirations. With the right approach, dedication, and perseverance, all students can find and win scholarships to help them achieve their goals.

Here is a list of scholarships available for non-minority white students, focusing on merit-based, need-based, and field-specific criteria:

General Merit-Based Scholarships
  1. Coca-Cola Scholars Program
  - Award: $20,000
  - Eligibility: High school seniors with a minimum GPA of 3.0, strong leadership, and community service.

2. Elks National Foundation Most Valuable Student Competition
  - Award: Up to $50,000
  - Eligibility: High school seniors who demonstrate leadership, academic excellence, and financial need.

3. Jack Kent Cooke Foundation College Scholarship Program
  - Award: Up to $40,000 per year
  - Eligibility: High-achieving high school seniors with financial need.

4. The Davidson Fellows Scholarship
  - Award: $50,000, $25,000, $10,000
  - Eligibility: Students 18 or younger who have completed a significant piece of work in science, technology, engineering,

mathematics, literature, music, philosophy, or outside the box.

Need-Based Scholarships
   5. Horatio Alger Association Scholarships
   - Award: Up to $25,000
   - Eligibility: High school seniors who have faced and overcome significant life obstacles and demonstrate financial need.

6. Pell Grants
   - Award: Varies (up to $6,495 for the 2023-2024 award year)
   - Eligibility: Undergraduate students with exceptional financial need.

Field-Specific Scholarships
   7. National Merit Scholarship Program
   - Award: $2,500
   - Eligibility: High school juniors who score highly on the PSAT/NMSQT.

8. The Barry Goldwater Scholarship
   - Award: Up to $7,500 per year
   - Eligibility: College sophomores and juniors pursuing research careers in natural sciences, mathematics, and engineering.

9. Microsoft Tuition Scholarship
   - Award: Full or partial tuition
   - Eligibility: Students pursuing computer science, engineering, or related STEM degrees

10. National Society Daughters of the American Revolution

(DAR) Scholarships
  - Award: Varies
  - Eligibility: Multiple scholarships are available for students with high academic achievement in various fields, including history, law, nursing, and more.

General Scholarships Open to All Students
  11. Burger King Scholars Program
  - Award: $1,000 to $50,000
  - Eligibility: High school seniors, Burger King employees, their dependent children, spouses, or domestic partners.

12. The Gates Scholarship
  - Award: Full cost of attendance
  - Eligibility: High school seniors from low-income households who demonstrate exceptional academic, leadership, and personal success.

13. AXA Achievement Scholarship
  - Award: Up to $25,000
  - Eligibility: High school seniors demonstrating ambition and self-drive, particularly as evidenced by outstanding achievement in school, community, or work-related activities.

Scholarships from Professional Organizations
  14. Society of Women Engineers (SWE) Scholarships
  - Award: Varies
  - Eligibility: Female students pursuing engineering degrees.

15. American Institute of CPAs (AICPA) Scholarships
  - Award: Varies

- Eligibility: Students pursuing a degree in accounting.

Community-Based Scholarships
   16. Local Rotary Club Scholarships
   - Award: Varies
   - Eligibility: Students demonstrating leadership and community service within their local area.

17. Chamber of Commerce Scholarships
   - Award: Varies
   - Eligibility: Students pursuing business-related degrees, often within the local community.

Byron-minority white students can find substantial financial support for their higher education endeavors. By exploring these scholarships and tailoring applications to each specific opportunity, remember to regularly check each scholarship's eligibility requirements and deadlines, as they vary.

Seventeen

CHAPTER 17 : SCHOLARSHIPS FOR MARGINALIZED COMMUNITIES

M inority scholarships are financial awards to support students from underrepresented or marginalized groups pursuing higher education. These scholarships aim to promote diversity and inclusion within academic institutions by financially assisting students facing systemic barriers to education. They can be based on various factors, including race, ethnicity, gender, sexual orientation, and more. Organizations, institutions, and foundations that value diversity and equality often fund these scholarships to help level the playing field and ensure that talented individuals from all backgrounds have the opportunity to succeed.

Finding minority scholarships involves a multi-faceted approach. Start by using scholarship search engines such as Fastweb, Scholarships.com, and Cappex, which allow you to filter results based on your specific minority status. Additionally, many professional organizations and advocacy groups offer scholarships tailored to their communities, such as the United Negro College Fund (UNCF) for African American students, the Hispanic Scholarship Fund (HSF) for Latino students, and the Asian & Pacific Islander American Scholarship Fund (APIASF). Consulting with high school guidance counselors, college financial aid offices, and community organizations can uncover valuable resources and opportunities.

Winning minority scholarships requires careful preparation and a robust application. Personalize each application to reflect how your experiences and aspirations align with the goals of the scholarship program. Highlight your academic achievements, leadership roles, community service, and any unique challenges you have overcome. Craft compelling personal essays that tell your story and demonstrate your commitment to positively impacting your community and beyond. Secure strong letters of recommendation from teachers, mentors, or community leaders who can attest to your qualifications and character. Attention to detail, meeting all deadlines, and following application instructions meticulously are also crucial for success.

Here is a list of notable minority scholarship opportunities:

1. United Negro College Fund (UNCF) Scholarships: Offers numerous scholarships for African American students across various fields of study.
2. Hispanic Scholarship Fund (HSF): Provides scholarships

to Latino students pursuing higher education in any discipline.

3. Asian & Pacific Islander American Scholarship Fund (APIASF): This fund supports Asian and Pacific Islander American students with scholarships for undergraduate education.
4. American Indian College Fund Scholarships: Offers financial assistance to Native American students attending tribal colleges or universities.
5. Gates Millennium Scholars Program: Provides full financial support for minority students demonstrating high academic achievement and leadership potential.
6. Thurgood Marshall College Fund (TMCF) Awards scholarships to students at historically black colleges and universities (HBCUs).
7. Point Foundation Scholarships: Supports LGBTQ+ students with scholarships based on academic excellence, leadership, and community involvement.
8. Jackie Robinson Foundation Scholarship: This scholarship offers financial assistance and mentoring to minority high school students who demonstrate leadership potential and dedication to community service.

By identifying and applying for these scholarships, students of color can access the financial resources needed to pursue their educational goals and significantly contribute to their communities.

Eighteen

CHAPTER 18: COMMUNITY COLLEGE SCHOLARSHIPS & TRANSFER SCHOLARSHIPS

C ommunity colleges offer an accessible and affordable pathway to higher education, making them an essential option for many students. They provide a wide range of programs that cater to various academic and career goals, allowing students to earn associate degrees, certificates, or credits that can be transferred to four-year institutions. Community colleges often have lower tuition than four-year colleges and universities, making education more financially manageable. Additionally, they tend to have flexible scheduling options, including evening and online classes, which benefit working students or those with family responsibilities. This accessibility and affordability make community colleges a crucial component of the higher education system, providing opportunities for students who might not otherwise be able to pursue post-secondary education.

For community college students, numerous scholarships are available to help cover tuition, books, and other expenses. These scholarships can significantly reduce financial burdens and allow students to focus more on their studies. Some scholarships are specific to community colleges, while others are open to all students but can be applied to community college expenses. Examples of community college scholarships include the Jack Kent Cooke Foundation Undergraduate Transfer Scholarship, which offers substantial financial support to high-achieving community college students who plan to transfer to four-year institutions. The Coca-Cola Community College Academic Team Program also provides scholarships to students who demonstrate academic excellence and leadership at their community colleges.

Transferring from a community college to a four-year institution is a common and strategic pathway for many students. To support this transition, various transfer scholarships are available that specifically cater to community college students moving to four-year colleges. These scholarships often recognize the unique challenges and achievements of transfer students. For example, the Phi Theta Kappa Transfer Scholarship is available to Phi Theta Kappa Honor Society members who are transferring to four-year institutions. Similarly, the Tau Sigma National Honor Society Scholarship supports transfer students who have excelled academically during their first semester at their new institution. These scholarships not only provide financial assistance but also recognize the academic success

71

and resilience of transfer students.

Here is a list of community college scholarships and transfer scholarships:

Community College Scholarships:
1. Jack Kent Cooke Foundation Undergraduate Transfer Scholarship
   - Award: Up to $40,000 per year
   - Eligibility: High-achieving community college students with financial need.

2. Coca-Cola Community College Academic Team Program
   - Award: Varies
   - Eligibility: Community college students demonstrating academic excellence and leadership.

3. American Association of Community Colleges (AACC) Scholarships
   - Award: Varies
   - Eligibility: Students attending AACC member colleges.

4. Community College Excellence Scholarship
   - Award: Varies
   - Eligibility: Students with exceptional academic performance and leadership at community colleges.

Transfer Scholarships:
5. Phi Theta Kappa Transfer Scholarship
   - Award: Varies (up to $2,500)
   - Eligibility: Phi Theta Kappa members transferring to four-

year institutions.

6. Tau Sigma National Honor Society Scholarship
   - Award: Varies
   - Eligibility: Transfer students who have excelled academically during their first semester at a four-year institution.

7. CollegeFish.org Transfer Scholarship
   - Award: Varies
   - Eligibility: Community college students using CollegeFish.org to plan their transfer to a four-year institution.

8. Transfer Regents Scholarship
   - Award: Varies
   - Eligibility: Community college transfer students to participating universities, often based on academic merit.

By taking advantage of these scholarships, community college students and transfer students can significantly reduce their educational costs, allowing them to focus on achieving their academic and career goals. Scholarships for community college and transfer students recognize the importance of these educational pathways and support students in successfully navigating their journeys to higher education.

Nineteen

CHAPTER 19 : INTERNATIONAL SCHOLARSHIPS

S cholarships for international students aspiring to study in the USA play a crucial role in making higher education accessible and affordable. These scholarships are designed to attract talented students worldwide, fostering diversity and cultural exchange within American colleges and universities. Many institutions, private organizations, and government bodies offer scholarships specifically for international students. These scholarships can cover a range of expenses, including tuition, living costs, travel, and books, thereby reducing the financial burden on students and enabling them to focus on their academic pursuits.

One of the primary sources of scholarships for international students is American universities. Many institutions offer merit-based scholarships to attract top global talent. For example, the Fulbright Foreign Student Program provides full scholarships to graduate students, young professionals, and artists from abroad to study and conduct research in the United States. Similarly, the Humphrey Fellowship Program offers non-degree scholarships for experienced professionals from designated countries undergoing development or political transition. Other universities, like Harvard, Stanford, and Yale, offer generous financial aid packages and scholarships to international students based on need and merit.

In addition to university scholarships, various private organizations and foundations offer scholarships specifically for international students. For instance, the Joint Japan World Bank Graduate Scholarship Program provides funding for students from developing countries to pursue graduate studies in development-related subjects. The Aga Khan Foundation International Scholarship Program offers scholarships for postgraduate studies to outstanding students from select developing countries who have no other means of financing their education. These scholarships provide financial support and often include mentorship and networking opportunities to help students succeed academically and professionally.

Here is a list of notable scholarships for international students wanting to study in the USA:

University-Based Scholarships:
1. Fulbright Foreign Student Program
- Award: Full funding for tuition, airfare, a living stipend, and health insurance.
- Eligibility: Graduate students and young professionals from

abroad.

2. Humphrey Fellowship Program
   - Award: Full funding for one year of non-degree graduate study.
   - Eligibility: Experienced professionals from designated countries.

3. Harvard University Scholarships
   - Award: Need-based financial aid for undergraduate and graduate international students.
   - Eligibility: Admitted international students demonstrating financial need.

4. Stanford University Scholarships
   - Award: Need-based financial aid for undergraduate international students.
   - Eligibility: Admitted international students demonstrating financial need.

Private Organization Scholarships:
   5. Joint Japan World Bank Graduate Scholarship Program
   - Award: Tuition, travel costs, and living stipend.
   - Eligibility: Students from developing countries pursuing graduate studies related to development.

6. Aga Khan Foundation International Scholarship Program
   - Award: Tuition and living expenses.
   - Eligibility: Outstanding students from select developing countries.

7. AAUW International Fellowships
   - Award: $18,000 to $30,000
   - Eligibility: Women from around the world pursuing graduate or postgraduate studies in the USA.

8. PEO International Peace Scholarship
   - Award: Up to $12,500
   - Eligibility: Women from other countries pursuing graduate studies in the USA.

9. Rotary Peace Fellowships
   - Award: Full funding for master's degrees in peace and conflict resolution.
   - Eligibility: Students from around the world.

By exploring these scholarship opportunities, international students can significantly reduce the financial challenges of studying in the USA. These scholarships provide crucial financial support and offer resources and networks to help international students succeed in their academic and professional endeavors.

Twenty

CHAPTER 20 : SCHOLARSHIPS FOR STUDENTS WITH DISABILITIES

~~~

S cholarships for students with disabilities are designed to provide financial support and promote educational opportunities for individuals who face unique challenges due to their physical, mental, or learning disabilities. These scholarships recognize the additional barriers students with disabilities often encounter in pursuing higher education, including increased medical expenses, accessibility needs, and specialized resources. These scholarships help alleviate some of the financial burdens by offering financial aid, allowing students to focus on their academic and personal growth.

Students with various types of disabilities are eligible for these scholarships. Disabilities may include, but are not limited to, physical disabilities such as mobility impairments, visual impairments, and hearing impairments; cognitive and learning disabilities such as dyslexia and ADHD; mental health conditions such as depression and anxiety; and chronic illnesses such as diabetes and epilepsy. Each scholarship may have specific criteria based on the type and severity of the disability and the applicant's academic and personal achievements.

Winning scholarships for students with disabilities requires highlighting strengths, achievements, and resilience. Applicants should focus on successfully managing their disability while pursuing their educational and career goals. Personal essays are critical, as they provide an opportunity to tell a compelling story about overcoming challenges and demonstrating perseverance. Strong letters of recommendation from teachers, mentors, or healthcare providers can bolster an application by providing additional perspectives on the student's capabilities and determination.

List of Scholarships for Students with Disabilities:

1. The AAHD Frederick J. Krause Scholarship on Health and Disability
   - Award: Varies
   - Eligibility: Undergraduate or graduate students with a disability pursuing studies related to health and disability.

2. The Google Lime Scholarship
   - Award: Up to $10,000
   - Eligibility: Students with disabilities pursuing a degree in computer science, engineering, or a related technical field.

3. Microsoft Disability Scholarship
   - Award: $5,000 per year
   - Eligibility: High school seniors with disabilities planning to attend a vocational or academic college and pursue a career in the technology industry.

4. The John Lepping Memorial Scholarship
   - Award: Up to $5,000
   - Eligibility: Students with disabilities residing in New York, New Jersey, or Pennsylvania.

5. The National Federation of the Blind Scholarship Program
   - Award: Varies (up to $12,000)
   - Eligibility: Legally blind students in the United States pursuing post-secondary education.

6. The Wells Fargo Scholarship Program for People with Disabilities
   - Award: Up to $2,500 for full-time students and $1,250 for half-time students
   - Eligibility: Students with disabilities enrolled in a two- or four-year institution in the United States.

7. The American Association on Health and Disability (AAHD) Scholarship
   - Award: $1,000
   - Eligibility: Students with disabilities pursuing undergraduate or graduate studies in a field related to health and disability.

8. The Autistic Self Advocacy Network (ASAN) Autistic Scholars Fellowship

- Award: $5,000
- Eligibility: Autistic students pursuing higher education.

9. The National Center for Learning Disabilities (NCLD) Anne Ford Scholarship
   - Award: $10,000
   - Eligibility: Graduating high school seniors with a documented learning disability or ADHD.

10. The Lighthouse Guild Scholarship
    - Award: Up to $10,000
    - Eligibility: Legally blind students pursuing post-secondary education.

These scholarships are instrumental in providing students with disabilities the financial support needed to pursue their educational aspirations. They not only help to cover tuition and related expenses but also recognize the unique strengths and contributions of students with disabilities. By applying for these scholarships, students can reduce their financial burdens and gain recognition for their achievements and resilience.

Twenty-One

CHAPTER 21 : SCHOLARSHIPS FOR NON-TRADITIONAL STUDENTS & ADULT LEARNERS

❧❧❧

Scholarships for non-traditional students and adult learners are designed to support individuals pursuing higher education later in life or non-traditional ways. These students often face unique challenges, such as balancing education with work and family responsibilities, returning to school after a significant gap, or pursuing education while managing other life commitments. Scholarships for non-traditional students provide essential financial assistance, making it more feasible for these individuals to achieve their academic and career goals without incurring excessive debt.

Non-traditional students may include adults returning to college after several years, working professionals seeking to advance their careers, single parents, military veterans, and individuals pursuing part-time or online education. These students bring diverse experiences and perspectives to the classroom, enriching the educational environment. Scholarships tailored to non-traditional students recognize these unique backgrounds and the paths leading to higher education. These scholarships help remove barriers and encourage lifelong learning and professional development by providing financial aid.

To win scholarships as a non-traditional student, applicants should emphasize their life experiences, goals, and the challenges they have overcome. Personal statements and essays are crucial to the application process, allowing candidates to share their stories and demonstrate their determination and commitment to education. Letters of recommendation from employers, community leaders, or educators can also strengthen applications by providing insight into the applicant's character, work ethic, and potential for success. Additionally, non-traditional students should leverage resources like academic advising and financial aid offices, which can guide available scholarships and application strategies.

List of Scholarships for Non-Traditional Students and Adult Learners:

1. Patsy Takemoto Mink Education Foundation Scholarship
   - Award: Up to $5,000
   - Eligibility: Low-income women with minor children pursuing education.

2. The Bernard Osher Foundation Reentry Scholarship Program
   - Award: Varies
   - Eligibility: Students who have experienced a cumulative gap in their education of five or more years and are now pursuing their first bachelor's degree.

3. The American Association of University Women (AAUW) Career Development Grants
   - Award: $2,000 to $12,000
   - Eligibility: Women pursuing a certificate or degree in a non-traditional field.

4. The Alpha Sigma Lambda Scholarship
   - Award: Varies
   - Eligibility: Non-traditional students who are members of Alpha Sigma Lambda, an honor society for adult learners.

5. The Soroptimist Live Your Dream Awards
   - Award: Up to $16,000
   - Eligibility: Women who provide the primary financial support for their families and are pursuing higher education.

6. The Imagine America Foundation Adult Skills Education Program (ASEP)
   - Award: $1,000
   - Eligibility: Adult learners attending participating career colleges.

7. Return2College Scholarship Program
   - Award: $1,000

- Eligibility: Adult students aged 17 or older who return to college.

8. The Jeannette Rankin Women's Scholarship Fund
   - Award: Varies
   - Eligibility: Low-income women, age 35 or older, pursuing a technical or vocational education, associate's degree, or first bachelor's degree.

9. The Kaplan University AASCU Scholarship
   - Award: Up to $10,000
   - Eligibility: Non-traditional students enrolled in Kaplan University's online programs.

10. The Unigo $10K Scholarship
    - Award: $10,000
    - Eligibility: Open to students age 13 or older, including non-traditional and adult learners.

These scholarships provide valuable financial assistance to non-traditional students and adult learners, helping them to overcome economic barriers and achieve their educational aspirations. By supporting this diverse group of students, these scholarships promote lifelong learning and contribute to developing a skilled and knowledgeable workforce.

Twenty-Two

CHAPTER 22: SCHOLARSHIPS FOR HIGH SCHOOL STUDENTS

Scholarships for high school students are critical in helping young learners transition smoothly into higher education. These scholarships are typically awarded based on a variety of criteria, including academic excellence, leadership qualities, community service involvement, athletic achievements, and specific talents or interests. Receiving a scholarship as a high school student not only provides financial relief but also boosts confidence and motivation, encouraging students to pursue their academic and career goals without the stress of financial constraints.

High school students can find scholarships through various sources, including local community organizations, national scholarship programs, private foundations, and educational institutions. Many scholarships are open to students from diverse backgrounds and interests, ensuring that every student has the opportunity to find an award that aligns with their unique profile. Guidance counselors, teachers, and online scholarship search engines are valuable resources for identifying these opportunities and understanding the application requirements.

To win scholarships, high school students should focus on highlighting their achievements, both academic and extracurricular, and crafting compelling personal statements or essays. Demonstrating a commitment to community service, leadership roles, and other extracurricular activities can significantly strengthen an application. Additionally, securing strong letters of recommendation from teachers, mentors, or community leaders can provide further support by attesting to the student's qualifications and character. Starting the scholarship search early and staying organized throughout the application process can increase the chances of success.

List of High School Scholarships for High School Students:

1. **Coca-Cola Scholars Program**
   - Award: $20,000
   - Eligibility: High school seniors with a minimum GPA of 3.0, leadership, and community service involvement.

2. **Gates Millennium Scholars Program**
   - Award: Full cost of attendance
   - Eligibility: High school seniors who are African American, American Indian/Alaska Native, Asian & Pacific Islander American, or Hispanic American, and who demonstrate academic excellence and leadership.

3. **Horatio Alger Scholarship**
   - Award: Up to $25,000
   - Eligibility: High school seniors who have faced and overcome significant obstacles and demonstrate financial need.

4. **Burger King Scholars Program**
   - Award: $1,000 to $50,000
   - Eligibility: High school seniors, Burger King employees, their dependent children, spouses, or domestic partners.

5. **The Davidson Fellows Scholarship**
   - Award: $50,000, $25,000, $10,000
   - Eligibility: Students 18 or younger who have completed a significant piece of work in science, technology, engineering, mathematics, literature, music, philosophy, or outside the box.

6. **The Prudential Spirit of Community Awards**
   - Award: Up to $5,000
   - Eligibility: High school students who have demonstrated exemplary community service.

7. **Jack Kent Cooke Foundation College Scholarship Program**
   - Award: Up to $40,000 per year
   - Eligibility: High-achieving high school seniors with financial need.

8. **Dell Scholars Program**
   - Award: $20,000
   - Eligibility: High school seniors participating in an approved college readiness program and demonstrating financial need.

9. **Elks National Foundation Most Valuable Student Competition**
   - Award: Up to $50,000
   - Eligibility: High school seniors demonstrating leadership, academic excellence, and financial need.

10. **National Merit Scholarship Program**
    - Award: $2,500
    - Eligibility: High school juniors who score highly on the PSAT/NMSQT.

These scholarships offer substantial financial support and recognition for high school students, enabling them to pursue higher education with fewer financial worries. By taking advantage of these opportunities, high school students can alleviate some of the financial burdens associated with college and set themselves up for academic and career success.

Twenty-Three

CHAPTER 23: SCHOLARSHIPS FOR COLLEGE STUDENTS

S cholarships for college students are crucial in helping to alleviate the financial burdens associated with higher education. As tuition costs continue to rise, these scholarships provide much-needed financial assistance to students already enrolled in college. They can cover various expenses, including tuition, books, supplies, and even living costs, enabling students to focus more on their studies and less on their financial concerns. Scholarships for college students can be merit-based, need-based, or specific to particular fields of study, extracurricular activities, or community involvement.

College students can access various scholarships through universities, private organizations, and professional associations. Merit-based scholarships often reward academic excellence, leadership skills, and extracurricular involvement, while need-based scholarships focus on students' financial situations. Additionally, many scholarships are available for students pursuing specific majors, such as engineering, business, or healthcare, and those participating in particular activities, like athletics, music, or community service. College students can find scholarships that align with their personal and academic profiles by exploring these opportunities.

Winning scholarships as a college student involves a strategic approach to the application process. Students should start by researching available scholarships and understanding the eligibility criteria and deadlines. Crafting a solid application is essential, including writing compelling personal statements or essays highlighting the applicant's achievements, goals, and unique qualities. Securing solid letters of recommendation from professors, advisors, or employers can also strengthen an application. Additionally, staying organized and keeping track of application deadlines ensures that students do not miss out on potential funding opportunities.

List of Scholarships for College Students:

1. The Barry Goldwater Scholarship
   - Award: Up to $7,500 per year
   - Eligibility: College sophomores and juniors pursuing research careers in natural sciences, mathematics, and engineering.

2. The Truman Scholarship
   - Award: Up to $30,000 for graduate study
   - Eligibility: College juniors demonstrating leadership poten-

tial and a commitment to public service.

3. The Udall Scholarship
   - Award: Up to $7,000
   - Eligibility: College sophomores and juniors committed to careers related to the environment, Native American health care, or tribal public policy.

4. The Beinecke Scholarship Program
   - Award: $34,000
   - Eligibility: College juniors planning to enter a research-focused master's or doctoral program in the arts, humanities, or social sciences.

5. The Boren Awards for International Study
   - Award: Up to $25,000
   - Eligibility: Undergraduate and graduate students planning to study abroad in areas critical to U.S. interests.

6. The National Science Foundation (NSF) Graduate Research Fellowship Program
   - Award: $34,000 per year for three years
   - Eligibility: Graduate students pursuing research-based master's and doctoral degrees in STEM fields.

7. The Point Foundation Scholarships
   - Award: Varies
   - Eligibility: LGBTQ+ students demonstrating academic excellence, leadership, and community involvement.

8. The Gilman International Scholarship Program

- Award: Up to $5,000
- Eligibility: Pell Grant recipients planning to study abroad.

9. The Society of Women Engineers (SWE) Scholarships
   - Award: Varies
   - Eligibility: Female students pursuing engineering degrees.

10. The American Institute of CPAs (AICPA) Scholarships
    - Award: Varies
    - Eligibility: Students pursuing a degree in accounting.

These scholarships offer substantial financial support to college students, allowing them to continue their education without the added stress of financial constraints. By taking advantage of these opportunities, students can focus on their academic and professional development, paving the way for a successful future.

Twenty-Four

CHAPTER 24: GRADUATE SCHOLARSHIPS

❧

Scholarships for graduate school are vital for students pursuing advanced degrees such as MBA, M.Ed, PhD, and EdD. These scholarships provide significant financial assistance, helping offset the high costs of graduate education, often including tuition, fees, research expenses, and living costs. Graduate scholarships are available from various sources, including universities, private organizations, professional associations, and government agencies. These scholarships enable students to focus on their studies and research without the burden of financial stress, allowing them to achieve their academic and professional goals.

There are several types of graduate scholarships that students can apply for. Merit-based scholarships are awarded based on academic excellence, leadership qualities, and professional achievements. Need-based scholarships provide financial aid to students who demonstrate financial need, helping to make graduate education accessible to those from lower-income backgrounds. Field-specific scholarships target students pursuing particular disciplines, such as business, education, or STEM fields. Additionally, research grants and fellowships are available for students engaged in significant research projects, offering funding for their research activities and expenses.

Finding graduate scholarships involves exploring multiple avenues. Universities often have their scholarship programs and fellowships for graduate students, which can be found on their financial aid or graduate school websites. Professional associations related to specific fields of study, such as the American Psychological Association (APA) for psychology students or the National Education Association (NEA) for education students, frequently offer scholarships and grants to support advanced education. Online scholarship databases and search engines, such as Fastweb, Scholarship.com, and GradSchools.com, allow students to search for scholarships tailored to their specific criteria and fields of study. Government agencies, such as the National Science Foundation (NSF) and the U.S. Department of Education, also provide grants and fellowships for graduate research and study.

List of Graduate Scholarships:

1. Fulbright Program
   - Award: Varies
   - Eligibility: Graduate students and professionals seeking to study, teach, or research abroad.

2. Rhodes Scholarship
   - Award: Full funding for study at the University of Oxford
   - Eligibility: Outstanding graduate students from around the world.

3. Knight-Hennessy Scholars Program
   - Award: Full funding for graduate study at Stanford University
   - Eligibility: Graduate students demonstrating leadership and innovation.

4. National Science Foundation (NSF) Graduate Research Fellowship Program
   - Award: $34,000 per year for three years
   - Eligibility: Graduate students pursuing research-based master's and doctoral degrees in STEM fields.

5. Paul & Daisy Soros Fellowships for New Americans
   - Award: Up to $90,000 over two years
   - Eligibility: Immigrants and children of immigrants pursuing graduate degrees in the United States.

6. AAUW International Fellowships
   - Award: $18,000 to $30,000
   - Eligibility: Women from around the world pursuing graduate or postgraduate studies in the USA.

7. MBA Fellowship Programs (e.g., Forte Foundation, Consortium for Graduate Study in Management)**
   - Award: Varies
   - Eligibility: MBA students demonstrating leadership poten-

tial and commitment to advancing diversity in business.

8. Phi Kappa Phi Fellowships
   - Award: Up to $35,000
   - Eligibility: Graduate students who are members of the Phi Kappa Phi honor society.

9. Ford Foundation Predoctoral Fellowship
   - Award: $27,000 per year for three years
   - Eligibility: PhD students from diverse backgrounds committed to a career in teaching and research.

10. GEM Fellowship Program
   - Award: Varies
   - Eligibility: Underrepresented minority students pursuing master's and doctoral degrees in engineering and science.

By actively seeking out and applying for these graduate scholarships, students can significantly reduce their financial burden and focus on academic and professional development. Utilizing university resources, professional associations, online databases, and government programs will help students find the funding they need to succeed in their advanced studies.

Twenty-Five

Conclusion

HOW TO OBTAIN A DEBT-FREE DEGREE

Embarking on the journey to obtain a debt-free degree is not only possible but also incredibly rewarding. Throughout this book, we have explored various strategies, tips, and resources that can help students secure the necessary financial aid to fund their education without incurring significant debt. By understanding the different types of scholarships available and mastering the application process, students can unlock numerous opportunities to support their academic aspirations. The journey requires diligence, perseverance, and a proactive approach, but the payoff is immeasurable.

Becoming a million-dollar scholar, like my children, is a testament to the power of dedication and strategic planning.

They demonstrated that starting early, maintaining a solid academic record, and actively participating in extracurricular activities make it possible to stand out in the competitive world of scholarships. Their success stories illustrate the importance of personalizing applications, crafting compelling narratives, and showcasing unique strengths and experiences. Any student can follow in their footsteps and achieve similar success by leveraging the resources and advice this book provides.

The key to obtaining a debt-free degree is thorough preparation and a relentless pursuit of available opportunities. This means continuously researching scholarships, staying organized with deadlines, and seeking support from mentors, counselors, and family. Utilizing the strategies outlined in this book, students can confidently navigate the complex landscape of financial aid. Whether through merit-based scholarships, need-based aid, or specialized awards for unique talents and backgrounds, a wealth of resources is available to help students reach their educational goals without the burden of debt.

In conclusion, the journey to becoming a million-dollar scholar is paved with opportunities for those willing to put in the effort and stay committed to their goals. With the right mindset and the tools provided in this book, you can secure the financial support needed to pursue your dreams and obtain a debt-free degree. Remember, each scholarship won is a step closer to achieving your academic and professional aspirations, and the knowledge and skills gained along the way will serve you well in all your future endeavors. By following these guidelines, you, too, can become a shining example of success and inspire others to embark on their scholarship journeys.

Afterword

I wrote this book and started my business to help students and families understand the scholarship process and earn a debt-free degree. I knew my information would be valuable to others, and I wanted to share it with the world.

I have to thank and dedicate this book to my family. Thank you to my husband, Cory, for supporting and believing in me. Thank you to my five fabulous children, Kay, Kiara, Taylor, Joe, and Liz, for inspiring my business and this book. I love you infinitely.

About the Author

Mrs. Laverne Mickens is a 24-year veteran educator, wife, mother of 5, and scholarship coach. She secured over $2 million in scholarships and grants for her five children, which are all debt-free. Her children are Hampshire College, Smith College, UMASS Amherst, and Holyoke Community College graduates. Her youngest daughter is a rising sophomore at Bard College with over $1M in grants and scholarships on her way to a debt-free degree. In 2023, she created "The Scholarship College Mama" to help other students and families obtain a debt-free degree.

Laverne and her work have been seen in USA Today and The Dr. Phil Show. Over the past year, her scholarship kids and clients have secured over $250,000 in scholarships.

You can connect with me on:

- https://stan.store/ScholarshipCollegeMama
- https://twitter.com/MrsMickens97
- https://www.facebook.com/laverne.mickens
- https://www.instagram.com/scholarshipcollegemama
- https://www.tiktok.com/@scholarshipcollegemama

Subscribe to my newsletter:

- https://open.substack.com/pub/lavernecollegescholarships/ p/summer-scholarship-winning?r=25o3hb&utm_campaign=post& utm_medium=web